Little Chimp
and Baby Chimp

Story by Jenny Giles
Illustrations by Rachel Tonkin

"Where is Mother Chimp?"
said Little Chimp.
"I can't find her."

Big Chimp said,

"Mother Chimp has gone

into the forest.

You can stay here

and play with your friends."

Little Chimp played
with his friends.
They played in the trees.

They got some food to eat.

Mother Chimp made her bed by Little Chimp.
Baby Chimp went to sleep with her.

Little Chimp went to sleep
in his new bed, up in the tree.

Then Little Chimp
looked for Mother Chimp again.
"Oh, where is she?" he said.

"Look!" said Big Chimp.
"Here she comes!"

Little Chimp ran
to see his mother.

Then he saw a baby chimp!

All the chimps

came to see Mother Chimp.

They patted her baby.

Little Chimp sat down
by his mother.

"I can help you
look after Baby Chimp,"
he said,
and he patted the baby, too.

The sun went down.

All the chimps went up

into the trees.

They made beds

to sleep in,

up in the trees.

Little Chimp said,

"I am big now.

I can make a bed

for myself

up in this tree."